The Arch

Biographies, Litanies, Chaplets,

Novena Prayers, and Powerful

Devotions to Archangels Michael,

Gabriel, and Raphael

Grace Mathew

Table of Contents

Introduction

In the realm between Heaven and Earth, where divine purpose meets human existence, there exist celestial beings of unparalleled significance. Among these luminous spirits, three archangels stand as stalwart guardians of light, messengers of God's will, and healers of the soul. Their names resonate with profound meaning and carry the weight of ages of devotion—Michael, Gabriel, and Raphael.

"The Archangels" invites you to embark on a journey into the celestial realm, delving deep into the lives, missions, and extraordinary grace of these three archangels. Within these pages, you will find a compilation of their biographies, litanies, chaplets, novena prayers, and powerful devotions, carefully curated to illuminate their roles as protectors, messengers, and healers.

As you turn these pages, you will come to know Michael, the valiant warrior archangel who vanquishes darkness and defends the faithful against evil's relentless assault. Discover Gabriel, the gentle herald, bearing divine messages and heralding the most extraordinary news in human history. And meet Raphael, the compassionate healer, whose touch brings solace to both body and soul.

These archangels have played pivotal roles in sacred scripture, tradition, and countless personal testimonies. Their unwavering dedication to humanity and their deep connection to the divine make them beloved figures in the spiritual journey of many. Each archangel possesses unique qualities, yet they all share a common mission—to guide, protect, and illuminate the path of those who seek their intercession.

This book serves as both an informative resource and a source of inspiration. Whether you are seeking guidance, healing, protection, or simply wish to deepen your connection with these heavenly beings, "Archangels: Guardians of Light and Grace" offers a wealth of prayers and devotions to help you forge a stronger bond with Michael, Gabriel, and Raphael.

You will discover not only the stories of these celestial messengers but also the profound impact they can have on your spiritual life. May this

compilation serve as a source of enlightenment,

faith, and devotion as you explore the awe-inspiring

presence of these archangels and their boundless

love for humanity.

Chapter 1: The Angelic Hierarchy

Around the fifth or sixth century, an influential theologian within the Church, referred to as Pseudo-Dionysius the Areopagite, drew upon the wealth of references found in Sacred Scriptures to elucidate the age-old comprehension of the angelic hierarchy. Building upon this foundation, Saint Thomas Aquinas, in the thirteenth century, further refined and expanded this doctrine. Both imparted the knowledge that this hierarchy is composed of nine choirs, organized into three triads. The highest triad, comprising the Seraphim, Cherubim, and Thrones, is wholly dedicated to ceaselessly worshiping God. The second triad, consisting of Dominions, Virtues, and Powers, governs the created world and the entire Universe. The third triad, which encompasses Principalities, Archangels, and Angels, maintains the closest proximity to humanity, acting as intermediaries who bridge the gap between God and humankind. Today, we pay homage to the Archangels within this celestial order.

Throughout the Old and New Testaments, celestial beings are frequently alluded to. In the Old Testament, they served as sentinels guarding the entrance to the Garden of Eden, guided and protected Abraham, intervened to save Isaac from harm, played pivotal roles in the destruction of Sodom, safeguarded Lot, engaged with Jacob in profound encounters, guided Moses and the Israelites through their journey, and conveyed divine messages to Israel's kings and prophets. In the New Testament, Archangel Gabriel took on the momentous task of heralding the births of both John the Baptist and Jesus. The teachings of Jesus Himself abound with references to the vital role played by angels. They provided solace to Him during His agonizing moments in the garden, bore witness to His Resurrection, and facilitated Peter's miraculous release from prison. Saint Paul, in his writings, also acknowledged the existence and order of the angelic hierarchy.

Saint Thomas Aquinas, the eminent theologian, expounded the doctrine that every individual is accompanied by a guardian angel. The archangels, occupying a significant position within the angelic hierarchy, are entrusted with the direct responsibility of serving humanity by fulfilling indispensable tasks. Although only three Archangels are explicitly mentioned in the Bible, earlier Jewish traditions acknowledged the presence of seven archangels, implying the potential involvement of numerous archangels in tending to crucial aspects of our lives. Among these celestial beings, Raphael identifies himself as one of the seven who stand in the divine presence.

Michael, bearing the name "Who is like God?," finds multiple references in the pages of Scripture. In the Book of Daniel, he emerges as the valiant defender and guardian of the people of Israel (Daniel 10:13, 10:21, and 12:1). The Letter of Jude recounts a significant episode wherein Michael confronts Satan in a dispute over the body of

Moses, with emphasis on Michael's choice not to issue judgment but rather to invoke the Lord's rebuke (Jude 1:9). The Book of Revelation vividly portrays Michael's pivotal role in a cosmic battle against Satan, leading to the expulsion of the adversary from the heavenly realm (Revelation 12:7–8). These passages firmly establish Michael's identity as the supreme defender against Satan and his demonic forces, the unwavering protector of the Church, and the exalted Prince among the Angels.

While Saint Thomas assigns him to the second lowest choir in the angelic hierarchy, other esteemed figures like Saints Basil, Robert Bellarmine, and Bonaventure have ventured to speculate that Michael commands the entire host of angels, occupying the position once held by Lucifer, the erstwhile light-bearer and a Seraphim of the highest order. The prayer to Saint Michael, invoking his divine defense in times of spiritual conflict, was composed by Pope Leo XIII and, until liturgical reforms following Vatican II, was recited at the conclusion of each Mass. Presently, it endures as a widely cherished prayer within numerous churches and personal devotions.

Gabriel, whose name signifies "God is my strength" or "Mighty Messenger of God," makes several notable appearances in the Bible. In the Book of Daniel, Gabriel serves as the interpreter of Daniel's profound visions (Daniel 8:15–27; 9:20–27).

Turning to the New Testament, we encounter Archangel Gabriel playing significant roles in delivering divine messages. He made a pivotal appearance to Zechariah within the sacred precincts of the Temple, announcing the upcoming birth of Zechariah's son, John the Baptist (Luke 1:5–20).

Equally momentous was Gabriel's visit to the Blessed Virgin Mary, bearing the extraordinary news of the impending birth of the Messiah (Luke 1:26–38). Some believe it was Gabriel who also conveyed divine guidance to Saint Joseph through a dream, alleviating his concerns about marrying Mary (Matthew 1:18–25). Consequently, Gabriel is often depicted in sacred artwork holding a trumpet, symbolizing his vital role in conveying divine messages, guiding prophets, and participating in significant events that shape human history.

Now, let's explore the figure of Raphael, whose name signifies "God has healed." Raphael is explicitly mentioned by name solely in the Book of Tobit. This book narrates the story of Tobit, a devout and prosperous Israelite who faced exile to Nineveh under the rule of the Assyrian king. During his exile, Tobit endured blindness and sent his son, Tobias, on a journey to recover his lost wealth. On this journey, Raphael appeared to Tobias in the guise of a human named Azariah. Raphael safeguarded Tobias throughout his expedition, leading him to Sarah, a woman who had tragically lost seven husbands on their wedding nights due to a malevolent demon. Raphael played a crucial role in uniting Tobias and Sarah in holy matrimony, vanquishing the demon, and safely guiding them back to Tobit. It was during this encounter that Raphael unveiled his true identity, declaring, "I am Raphael, one of the seven angels who stand and serve before the Glory of the Lord" (Tobit 12:15).

Additionally, some speculate that Raphael may be among the seven angels mentioned in the Book of Revelation, each entrusted with one of the seven trumpets (Revelation 8:2).

While the complete nature and purpose of these angelic beings remain veiled in mystery, one truth shines clearly: God has utilized them significantly throughout the course of salvation history. Even in the present day, we can confidently affirm that God continues to shower His grace upon us through the agency of angels, with a special emphasis on Archangels Michael, Gabriel, and Raphael. God chose to disclose their names to us, inviting us to seek their intercession. These archangels are not mere intermediaries; they bear the responsibility of executing God's divine will.

As we commemorate these three archangels today, we are encouraged to invoke their intercession, place our trust in their mediation, and have faith that they diligently carry out their divine tasks. Through Michael, we seek God's protective embrace. Through Gabriel, we long for God's divine revelations. Through Raphael, we implore God's healing touch. These archangels stand unwavering in the fulfillment of their roles.

Glorious Archangels Michael, Gabriel, and Raphael, we rely on your angelic mediation. We implore you to set into motion God's divine plan for our lives, to safeguard us from the traps of the evil one, to convey God's holy message to our hearts, and to heal us from our spiritual afflictions. We offer our heartfelt gratitude for the crucial responsibilities you undertake in God's divine mission. Saints Michael, Gabriel, and Raphael, we earnestly request your prayers and mediation. Jesus, we place our trust in You.

Chapter 2: Saint Michael the Archangel

Saint Michael the Archangel, known as "Who resembles God?," occupies a significant position in the celestial hierarchy. His name served as the battle cry of the loyal angels during the celestial conflict against the adversary and his followers. The Scriptures make mention of Saint Michael on four occasions:

1. In the book of Daniel (Daniel 10:13 and following), Archangel Gabriel discloses that Michael, one of the principal leaders, came to assist him in his mission to petition for the Jews' return to Jerusalem.

2. In another part of the Book of Daniel (Daniel 12), the Archangel speaks of Michael's role as the grand prince who will emerge during the final days, defending the offspring of God's chosen people.

3. St. Jude's Catholic Epistle alludes to a disagreement between Michael and the devil regarding Moses' remains, referencing an ancient Jewish tradition. This account appears in the apocryphal text concerning Moses' assumption, and it's notable that Saint Michael concealed Moses' tomb.

4. In the book of Revelation (Apocalypse 12:7), Saint John portrays a momentous celestial battle where Michael and his angelic host confront the

dragon. This confrontation symbolizes the ultimate struggle that will transpire at the culmination of time, echoing the celestial clash that transpired at the dawn of creation.

In addition to these explicit references, early Christian tradition hints at Saint Michael's presence in Scripture going beyond these instances. Certain traditions identify him as the cherub who guarded the entrance to paradise (Genesis 3:24), the angel who delivered the Commandments to God's chosen people, the angel who stood against Balaam (Numbers 22:22 and following), and the angel who routed Sennacherib's army (2 Kings 19:35).

Considering these biblical passages, Christian tradition attributes four significant roles to Saint Michael:

1. Engaging in battle against Satan.

2. Safeguarding the souls of the faithful from the clutches of the adversary, especially during the moment of passing into the afterlife.

3. Serving as the defender of God's people, both in the Old Covenant, representing the Jewish community, and in the New Testament, as a guardian of Christians. Consequently, he emerged as the patron of the Church and chivalrous orders during the medieval era.

4. Summoning departed souls from their earthly existence to face divine judgment.

In terms of Saint Michael's position within the celestial hierarchy, viewpoints differ. Some, like Saint Basil and specific Greek Church Fathers, as well as theologians such as Salmeron and Bellarmine, designate him as the foremost among all angels, bearing the designation "archangel" because of his role as the leader of the other angels. Conversely, others, following the beliefs of Saint Bonaventure, assert that he presides over the seraphim, the loftiest order of angels. Saint Thomas Aquinas, on the other hand, assigns him leadership over the lowest choir, the angels.

Within the Roman Liturgy, Saint Michael is often acknowledged in alignment with the views of the Greek Church Fathers as the "Princeps militia coelestis," signifying the principal figure among the heavenly forces. The Mozarabic Breviary even elevates his status above that of the Twenty-four Elders.

The veneration of Saint Michael has a rich history, evolving over time. Initially, early Christians looked to certain martyrs like St. George and St. Theodore as patrons for military matters. However, St. Michael's connection with healing, especially in Phrygia, transformed him into a guardian of the sick and a central figure in the worship of the holy angels.

According to tradition, in ancient times, St. Michael performed a miraculous act, causing a healing spring to burst forth near Colossae, known as Chairotopa. Those who bathed in this spring while invoking the Blessed Trinity and St. Michael experienced remarkable healings.

Even more famous are the springs linked to St. Michael in Colossae, known as Chonae, located in present-day Khonas, along the Lycus River. Pagan adversaries once directed a stream against the sanctuary of St. Michael to destroy it. However, the archangel intervened, splitting the rock with a lightning bolt to create a new course for the stream, forever sanctifying the waters. The Greeks celebrate this apparition on 6 September, and it holds significance in Pythia (Bithynia) and other parts of Asia where hot springs are dedicated to St. Michael.

In Constantinople, St. Michael was esteemed as the celestial physician. His main sanctuary, the Michaelion, was situated about fifty miles south of the city in Sosthenion. It was here that the archangel was believed to have appeared to Emperor Constantine. The sick would spend the night in this church, hoping for a manifestation of St. Michael. His feast was celebrated on 9 June. Another noteworthy church within Constantinople's walls was located at Emperor Arcadius' thermal baths. Here, the synaxis of the archangel was observed on 8 November. This feast extended its influence across the Greek Church and was adopted by the Syrian, Armenian, and Coptic Churches, becoming the primary feast of St. Michael in the Orient. While its roots may be traced back to Phrygia, its focal point in Constantinople was the Thermae of Arcadius.

In Egypt, Christians placed the life-giving Nile River under St. Michael's protection and embraced the Greek feast on 12 November. Every twelfth day of the month, they commemorated the archangel, with 12 June holding special significance as a holiday of obligation dedicated to St. Michael "for the rising of the Nile," known as "euche is ten symmetron anabasine ton potion hydration."

In the annals of Rome, the Leonine Sacramentary hailing from the sixth century acknowledged the "Natale Basilicae Angeli via Salaria" on the 30th of

September, featuring St. Michael prominently in three out of five Masses for this occasion. The Gelasian Sacramentary, dating back to the seventh century, marked the feast as "S. Michaelis Archangeli." In the eighth century, the Gregorian Sacramentary referred to it as "Dedicatio Basilionis S. Angeli Michaelis" on the 29th of September, with a manuscript appending "via Salaria" to its name. The church in question, the Basilica Archangeli, resided six miles north of the city and, in the ninth century, became renowned as "St. Michaelis inter nubes" (in Summit circa).

A momentous apparition of St. Michael unfolded on the 8th of May, with historical roots stretching back to either the year 494 or 530-40. This event, commemorated in the Roman Breviary, took place on Monte Gargano, where St. Michael's original role as a patron in times of warfare was reaffirmed. In 663, the Lombards of Sipontum (Manfredonia) attributed their victory over the Greek Neapolitans to St. Michael on the 8th of May. In honor of this triumph, the church of Sipontum established a special feast dedicated to the archangel on the same date, known as "Apparitio S. Michaelis." Although this feast has since spread throughout the Latin Church, its origins initially commemorated the victory rather than the apparition itself.

In Normandy, the renowned sanctuary of Mont-Saint-Michel, nestled in the Diocese of Coutances, recognizes St. Michael as the patron of mariners. Legend has it that St. Michael appeared at this hallowed site in 708 to St. Aubert, the Bishop of

Avranches. Historically, the people of Normandy celebrated his feast, known as "S. Michaelis in periculo maris" or "in Monte Tumba," universally on the 18th of October. This date marked the anniversary of the initial church's dedication on the 16th of October in 710. Presently, this feast primarily finds observance within the Diocese of Coutances.

In Germany, following its conversion to Christianity, St. Michael assumed a prominent role, replacing the pagan god Wotan, associated with numerous sacred mountains. This transition led to the construction of numerous mountain chapels dedicated to St. Michael across Germany.

The hymns attributed to St. Rabanus Maurus of Fulda (d. 856) within the Roman Office are closely associated with St. Michael. In artistic representations, St. Michael is commonly depicted as an angelic warrior, fully armored with a helmet, sword, and shield. The shield often bears the Latin inscription: "Quis ut Deus," underscoring his divine nature. He is frequently depicted triumphing over a vanquished dragon, sometimes piercing it with a lance. In other depictions, St. Michael holds a pair of scales for weighing the souls of the departed or the book of life, symbolizing his role in the judgment of souls.

During the medieval era, St. Michael's feast day, celebrated on the 29th of September, held the status of a holy day of obligation. Nevertheless, in the eighteenth century, along with several other feasts, its mandatory observance gradually waned. In England and various other countries, Michaelmas Day retained significance as one of the regular quarter-days for settling rents and accounts.

Nonetheless, it no longer enjoys the same renown for hospitality and festivities that once characterized it. In some parishes, such as the Isle of Skye, traditions included processions and the baking of a special cake known as "St. Michael's bannock" on this day.

Chapter 3: Saint Gabriel the Archangel

Saint Gabriel the Archangel stands out as a celestial messenger of God, a revered figure in the Catholic Bible acknowledged by name among the trio of angels.

Gabriel's remarkable appearances encompass:

1. A visitation to the prophet Daniel, where he provided profound insights into Daniel's visions pertaining to the Messiah. (Daniel 8:16-26; 9:21-27)

2. A divine manifestation within the temple, where Gabriel conveyed the remarkable news to Zechariah

about the impending birth of John the Baptist to him and his wife Elizabeth. Regrettably, Zechariah's disbelief led to a temporary loss of his ability to speak. (Luke 1:11-20)

3. The most iconic appearance, perhaps, was to the Virgin Mary, bearing tidings that she had been chosen as the vessel to bring forth the Saviour. (Luke 1:26-38)

In the realm of theology, it's crucial to recognize that the term "angel" denotes a role rather than a distinct nature. These celestial entities have perpetually existed as spirits, assuming the title of angels when they convey divine messages. Among this celestial assembly, those who bear messages of lesser magnitude are referred to as angels, while archangels are entrusted with conveying messages of paramount importance.

In a homily, Pope Saint Gregory the Great underscored the profound significance of Gabriel's role as the archangel entrusted with delivering the most momentous message of all—the revelation of the Messiah's birth. The name Gabriel, meaning "God's strength," aptly befitted his task as the herald of the arrival of the Lord of heavenly dominions, a divine warrior who would, in humility, confront cosmic forces to achieve victory.

Further illumination regarding Gabriel's role unfolds within the Book of Daniel. When Daniel discerned a human voice invoking Gabriel to elucidate a vision, he was overcome with awe.

Gabriel, in turn, deciphered that this vision pertained to the culmination of times, unraveling the cryptic significance of diverse symbols and forthcoming events. These revelations encompassed the ascent and decline of empires, the emergence of a shrewd and audacious monarch, and divine intervention against the "prince of princes."

In Zechariah's rendezvous with Gabriel, we glimpse the angel's manifestation at the right side of the incense altar within the temple's sacred precincts. Despite Zechariah's initial trepidation, Gabriel tenderly reassured him that his supplications had resonated, and his wife Elizabeth would bear a son named John.

During the sixth month, the celestial envoy Gabriel received divine commission to journey to the town of Nazareth in Galilee. There, he approached a young maiden named Mary, betrothed to Joseph, a descendant of David. In his salutation, Gabriel uttered, "Rejoice, favored one! The Lord is with you." Understandably, Mary was perplexed by this extraordinary greeting, contemplating its profound import.

Gabriel, sensing her disquiet, offered solace, saying, "Fear not, Mary, for you have discovered favor with God. Behold, you shall conceive in your womb and bring forth a son, whom you shall name Jesus. He shall be renowned as the Son of the Most High. The Lord God will bestow upon him the throne of his forefather David, and his reign over the house of

Jacob shall endure eternally, with a kingdom unbounded by time."

In a humble pursuit of clarity, Mary inquired, "How shall this be, since I have not known a man?"

In response, the angel Gabriel unveiled the miraculous design: "The Holy Spirit shall descend upon you, and the might of the Most High shall overshadow you. Thus, the child to be born shall be hailed as holy, the Son of God. Even your kinswoman Elizabeth, once deemed barren, now carries a child in her sixth month, for nothing is beyond God's omnipotence."

With unwavering faith and submission, Mary declared, "Behold, I am the handmaiden of the

Lord. May it be done to me according to your utterance." In this profound acquiescence to the divine plan, the angel departed, leaving Mary to contemplate the extraordinary announcement that heralded the imminent birth of Jesus, the Redeemer. Gabriel's role as the bearer of God's messages underscores the miraculous unfolding of events, where the inconceivable becomes a reality through divine intervention.

Chapter 4: Saint Raphael the Archangel

Saint Raphael the Archangel, also known as Azariah, is celebrated as the Angel of Compassion and Delight. He occupies a prominent station among the celestial beings, being one of the three angels explicitly mentioned in the sacred Scriptures and counted among the seven who stand in the august presence of God's throne.

In the deutero-canonical book of Tobit, we are graced with the extraordinary account of Saint Raphael. Disguised in the semblance of a mortal, he takes on the role of a loyal and protective companion to the young Tobias, introducing himself as "Azarias, the offspring of the illustrious Ananias." Their journey unfolds, laden with trials, including the miraculous healing of a man's blindness and the binding of a malevolent demon. Saint Raphael's benevolent influence permeates every facet of this narrative, particularly in his capacity as the guardian of sojourners, the patron of youth, and the wellspring of healing and counsel for those in the healing arts.

Within this book, Saint Raphael's name, which signifies "God has brought healing," is unveiled. His true identity is divulged when, after the conclusion of their eventful expedition and the restoration of the elder Tobias's sight, he reveals himself as "the angel Raphael, one of the seven who stand in the presence of the Lord" (Tobit 12:15). It is noteworthy that these seven archangels are an acknowledged component of post-Exilic Jewish angelology, with Gabriel, Michael, and Raphael being the sole trio mentioned in the canonical Scriptures.

Saint Raphael's principal roles, as narrated in the Book of Tobit, encompass presenting prayers to the Almighty while Tobias engages in acts of compassion and charity. His divine mission encompasses the miraculous healing of Tobias's blindness and the liberation of Sara, his son's bride, from the clutches of malevolent forces.

While Saint Raphael's name does not explicitly appear in the New Testament, some scholars link him to the "angel of the Lord" referenced in John 5, given the profound significance of his name and his curative role in the Book of Tobit.

The Church venerates Saint Raphael on the 24th day of October. The hymns woven into the Office on this sacred occasion accentuate his role as a healer and his triumphant victory over sinister forces. Lessons extracted from the Book of Tobias and the writings of St. Augustine are integral to the liturgical commemoration, affirming Saint Raphael's exalted position among the heavenly assembly as a source of divine healing and counsel.

Chapter 5: Litany To The Divine Archangels, St. Michael, St. Gabriel & St. Raphael.

Lord, in Your boundless mercy, heed our plea.

Christ, in Your tender mercy, heed our plea.

Lord, in Your infinite mercy, heed our plea.

Christ, graciously hear us.

O God, Father of the heavenly realms, Creator of all ethereal beings,

have compassion upon us.

O God, Son, Redeemer of the world, the desire of
angelic hosts,

have compassion upon us.

O God, Holy Spirit, source of bliss for the blessed
spirits,

have compassion upon us.

Blessed Trinity, one God, resplendence of the
angelic legions,

have compassion upon us.

Blessed Mary, Queen of angelic choirs,

intercede for us.

St. Michael, sovereign of celestial forces,

intercede for us.

Leader of the angels of serenity,

intercede for us.

Mighty in celestial strife,

intercede for us.

Vanquisher of the age-old serpent,

intercede for us.

Guardian forever of God's people,

intercede for us.

Who cast out Lucifer and his rebellious followers

from Heaven's realm,

intercede for us.

Who guides departing souls to the gates of Paradise,

intercede for us.

Comfort of the faithful,

intercede for us.

Patron of the devoted to your guardianship,

intercede for us.

St. Gabriel, revealer of divine mysteries to Daniel,

intercede for us.

Herald of the birth and mission of St. John the

Baptist,

intercede for us.

Bearer of the message of the Word's Incarnation,

intercede for us.

Guardian of the Holy Virgin,

intercede for us.

Witness to the Saviour's infant days,

intercede for us.

Solace to Christ in His hour of agony,

intercede for us.

Faithful servant of Christ,

intercede for us.

St. Raphael, angelic source of healing,

intercede for us.

St. Raphael, among the seven who stand before the Throne,

intercede for us.

Loyal guide to Tobias,

intercede for us.

Who banished the devil in the name of the Lord,

intercede for us.

Presenter of our prayers before the Divine,

intercede for us.

Healer of blindness,

intercede for us.

Aid in times of tribulation,

intercede for us.

Comforter in moments of need,

intercede for us.

Bringing joy to your devoted servants,

intercede for us.

Holy Michael, Gabriel, and Raphael,

intercede for us.

Lord Jesus Christ, ultimate bliss of the angelic host,

spare us.

Lord Jesus Christ, glory of the heavenly spirits,

hear us.

Lord Jesus Christ, radiance of the celestial armies,

have mercy on us.

To St. Michael

O God, who exalted blessed Michael, your

archangel,

to triumph over the haughty Lucifer and the

malevolent spirits,

we implore you to grant us victory under the banner

of the Cross,

embracing his motto 'Who is like God?'

May we conquer all adversities and be freed from

every obstacle,

and may our lives be guided by your divine will and

commandments.

Through Jesus Christ, our Lord.

Amen.

To St. Gabriel

O God, the lover of humanity's salvation,

who commissioned blessed Gabriel to stand in Your

presence,

announcing to the ever-glorious Virgin the mystery

of Your blessed Son's incarnation,

we beseech You,

that by seeking his intercession,

we may find assistance in all our needs, both

spiritual and temporal.

Through Jesus Christ, our Lord.

Amen.

To St. Raphael

O God, in your infinite goodness,

you made blessed Raphael the guide of your faithful

during their journeys.

We humbly ask that he may lead us on the path of

salvation

and provide us with aid in the afflictions of our

souls.

Through Jesus Christ, our Lord.

Amen.

Act Of Consecration

Most noble Prince of the Angelic Hierarchies,

courageous champion of Almighty God,

and zealous defender of His glory,

terror to the rebellious angels,

and joy of all the righteous,

my beloved Archangel Saint Michael,

desiring to be counted among your devoted
servants,

I consecrate myself, along with my family,

and all my possessions, under your powerful

protection.

I humbly ask that you do not consider the

insignificance of my offering,

as I am but a wretched sinner,

but instead, look favorably upon the heartfelt

devotion with which I make this dedication.

Remember that from this day forward,

I am under your patronage,

and I ask for your assistance throughout my life,

obtaining forgiveness for my numerous grave

offenses and sins.

I pray for the grace to love my God, my Savior

Jesus,

and my Blessed Mother Mary with all my heart,

and I seek your help in attaining my ultimate reward

in glory.

Defend me against my spiritual adversaries,

especially during my final moments on this earthly

journey.

Come, glorious Prince, and support me in my last

battle,

using your mighty weapon to cast far from me that

deceitful and prideful angel

whom you once humbled in the celestial conflict.

Saint Michael, protect us in our daily struggles,

so that we may not be lost in the final Judgment.

Chapter 6: Novena Prayers to the Archangels

Why Turn to Novenas for Intercession by Saints?

Novenas, those nine-day prayer traditions, offer a distinctive channel for seeking the intercession of saints. You might wonder, though, why engage in this particular form of prayer? Let's explore the profound reasons that underlie the practice of novenas.

Firstly, seeking the intercessory prayers of saints in itself is a potent spiritual practice. These holy individuals, now in the presence of God, share a unique connection with the Divine. By seeking their assistance, we tap into this spiritual network, linking us to God through their steadfast devotion.

However, novenas elevate this practice. Praying with the saints for nine consecutive days, with a specific intention, is not only beautiful but also commendable. It signifies our commitment to persistent prayer, mirroring the saints' own determination in their spiritual journeys.

Furthermore, novenas offer a precious opportunity to discover more about the particular saint we invoke. Over these nine days of devotion, we gain insights into their lives, their stories, and the virtuous acts they performed. This deepens our bond with the saint and allows us to draw inspiration from their exemplary lives.

It's essential to recognize that saints represent the pinnacle of human virtue and unwavering devotion to God. The Catholic Church officially recognizes them due to their extraordinary holiness. During their earthly existence, they centered their lives on Christ and served God with unwavering dedication, setting a profound example for all of humanity.

Their ultimate purpose was to bring glory to God, and now, in God's presence, they continue to intercede on our behalf. Their selfless devotion and perfect love shine through their desire to see us join them in the eternal bliss of Heaven. By asking for their prayers to meet our needs, we align ourselves with these spiritual giants, making a wise choice in seeking divine favor.

The prayers of the saints hold a unique and remarkable potency. Their selflessness and unwavering faith grant their prayers great influence in the heavenly realms. When we seek their intercession, we essentially leverage their merits to reinforce our own petitions to God.

Another compelling reason to turn to the saints lies in their steadfast dedication to God's noblest purpose. Throughout their lives, God remained at the forefront of their every action. Their choices consistently prioritized God over personal gain, fame, worldly honors, and favors. By aligning ourselves with the saints through prayer, we draw closer to their noble mission — to seek, follow, and wholeheartedly love God.

In essence, establishing a prayerful connection with the saints allows us to link with individuals who embody the virtues and values we aspire to. Their prayers and companionship become potent allies in our spiritual journey, offering invaluable guidance and support.

So, in times of need, it is not just prudent but profoundly advantageous to seek the company of these holy companions. They have traversed the path of unwavering faith, and through novenas and prayers, we can walk alongside them toward the same divine light.

How to Approach a Novena with Sincerity

Engaging in a novena is a straightforward yet deeply meaningful practice. There is no need for strict regulations like praying at specific hours, fasting, or incorporating the rosary into your novena. It's vital to understand that novenas are not akin to magical spells that guarantee the fulfillment of our desires. We should recognize that God, our Heavenly Father, ultimately holds sovereignty, and we do not exert control over Him. He is not a wish-granting genie but a loving and all-knowing God.

As Christians, we often pray, "Your will be done," acknowledging that God's plan surpasses our understanding, even if we cannot always comprehend it. Therefore, we are free to request good things, but we should trust that God knows what is best for us. Exercise caution with novenas that make specific promises or employ threats for non-compliance, as these can resemble chain letters and should be approached with discernment.

Nonetheless, it is worth noting that Jesus encourages us to engage in frequent prayer in the Bible, and a novena can serve as a valuable tool for enriching our prayer life.

What If You Miss a Day in Your Novena?

Do not worry if you find yourself missing a day during your novena; there are several options available:

1. You can simply skip the missed day and continue with the novena.
2. Alternatively, you may choose to say two daily prayers on the same day to catch up.
3. If you prefer, you can say the prayer you missed and continue your novena one day behind the schedule of others.

The choice is entirely yours, and there are no rigid rules or negative consequences for missing a day. Remember, God is merciful and forgiving.

Can You Pray for the Same Thing or Something Different Each Day?

You have the freedom to approach your novena in either of these ways. What truly matters is that your prayers are sincere, heartfelt expressions of your desires, and that you remain open to whatever God's divine plan holds for you.

In conclusion, let us approach novenas with authenticity, recognizing that God's wisdom transcends our understanding. With faith, trust, and heartfelt prayer, we can draw closer to Him, seeking

His guidance, blessings, and grace.

"Dear Jesus, whose Heart overflows with love,

kindness, obedience, patience, and care, I offer this

novena in gratitude. Please grant me the grace I

seek. Amen."

Chapter 7: Novena prayers to Saint Michael the Archangel

Day 1

In the name of the Father, the Son, and the Holy Spirit.

Amen.

St. Michael, Archangel of exceptional valor, we hold you in the highest regard as a steadfast guardian of the Church and our souls. Your beacon of humility, courage, and unwavering strength shines brightly, urging us to turn away from sin and embrace our love for our Heavenly Father.

With your unparalleled strength and profound humility, we implore you to vanquish the malevolence and arrogance that may dwell within our hearts, ensuring that no obstacle shall separate us from God.

St. Michael, we earnestly request your intercession on our behalf, that God may bless us with the fervor to lead our lives in accordance with Christ's teachings.

You, the distinguished prince among angels, exemplified humility by acknowledging God's supremacy and embracing your role as His devoted servant. Unlike the fallen angel, Satan, who succumbed to pride, you remained steadfast in your humility. We beseech you to guide us in cultivating this same humility in our lives.

With hearts steeped in humility, we present our petitions...

(State your petitions)

"Saint Michael the Archangel, be our defender in the midst of spiritual battles, shielding us from the malevolence and snares of the devil. May God, in His boundless mercy, rebuke him, we fervently pray; and by divine power, cast Satan and all malevolent spirits into the depths of hell, where they seek the destruction of souls."

Amen.

In the name of the Father, the Son, and the Holy Spirit.

Amen.

Day 2

In the name of the Father, the Son, and the Holy Spirit.

Amen.

St. Michael the Archangel, we honor your unwavering guardianship over the Church and our souls. Your radiant example of humility, courage, and indomitable strength inspires us to turn away from sin and cultivate a profound love for our Heavenly Father.

With your mighty strength and profound humility, we implore you to conquer the shadows of evil and pride that may linger within our hearts, allowing us to draw nearer to God's divine presence.

St. Michael the Archangel, we beseech you to intercede on our behalf, that we may be graced with the ability to recognize the divine image of God in the least of our brothers and sisters.

You, the noble prince of angels, exemplified humility by acknowledging God's supremacy and embracing your role as His devoted servant. Unlike Satan, who succumbed to pride, you remained unwavering in your humility. We earnestly seek your guidance in nurturing this same humility within our own lives.

With hearts grounded in humility, we present our petitions...

(State your petitions)

"Saint Michael the Archangel, stand as our defender in the face of spiritual battle, shielding us from the malevolence and snares of the devil. May God, in His infinite mercy, rebuke him, we fervently pray; and by divine power, cast Satan and all malevolent spirits into the depths of hell, where they seek the destruction of souls."

Amen.

In the name of the Father, the Son, and the Holy Spirit.

Amen.

Day 3

In the name of the Father, the Son, and the Holy Spirit.

Amen.

St. Michael the Archangel, we offer our tribute to your unwavering guardianship over the Church and our very souls. Your resolute humility, unyielding bravery, and enduring strength illuminate our path, encouraging us to turn away from sin and embrace our love for our Heavenly Father.

With your unparalleled strength and profound humility, we implore you to vanquish the shadows of evil and pride concealed within the depths of our hearts, ensuring that no barriers remain between us and God's grace.

St. Michael the Archangel, we earnestly seek your intercession, guarding us from the cunning snares of the adversary and guiding us away from treacherous paths of sin.

You, the distinguished prince among angels, epitomize humility through your unwavering acknowledgment of God's supreme authority and your wholehearted embrace of your role as His devoted servant. Unlike Satan, who succumbed to the blinding allure of pride, you remained steadfast in your humility. We fervently pray for your guidance in nurturing this same virtue within our own lives.

With hearts humbled by the spirit of humility, we present our petitions before you...

(State your petitions)

"Saint Michael the Archangel, stand as our valiant defender in the face of spiritual battle, become our impenetrable shield against the wickedness and crafty snares of the devil. We humbly beseech God to rebuke him; and by the boundless power of God, may you, O Prince of the Heavenly host, cast Satan and all malevolent spirits into the abyss of hell, where they relentlessly seek the ruin of souls."

Amen.

In the name of the Father, the Son, and the Holy
Spirit.

Amen.

Day 4

In the name of the Father, the Son, and the Holy Spirit.

Amen.

St. Michael the Archangel, we hold you in profound reverence as a formidable protector of the Church and the vigilant guardian of our souls. May your unwavering humility, undaunted courage, and enduring strength serve as a wellspring of inspiration, compelling us to cast aside sin and embrace a deeper love for our Heavenly Father.

With your indomitable strength and unwavering humility, we beseech you to vanquish the lurking evil and pride concealed within our hearts, ensuring that no chasm separates us from the loving embrace of God.

St. Michael the Archangel, we earnestly implore your divine intercession, that we may be graced with an unyielding desire to humble ourselves before the Almighty and willingly surrender to His divine will.

You, the distinguished prince among angels, epitomize the virtue of humility through your unswerving acknowledgment of God's supreme authority and your wholehearted embrace of your role as His devoted servant. Unlike Satan, who succumbed to the blinding allure of pride, you remained steadfast in your humility. We humbly pray that you may guide us in nurturing and cultivating this same profound humility in our own lives.

With hearts steeped in the spirit of humility, we present our petitions before you...

(State your petitions)

"Saint Michael the Archangel, stand as our valiant defender in the midst of our spiritual battles; be our impenetrable shield against the malevolence and cunning snares of the devil. We humbly beseech God to rebuke him; and through the boundless power of God, may you, O Prince of the Heavenly host, cast Satan and all malevolent spirits into the abyss of hell, where they relentlessly seek the ruin of souls."

Amen.

In the name of the Father, the Son, and the Holy Spirit.

Amen.

Day 5

In the name of the Father, and of the Son, and the Holy Spirit.

Amen.

St. Michael the Archangel, we offer our reverence for your role as a mighty protector of the Church and the vigilant guardian of our souls. May your humility, courage, and strength be an everlasting source of inspiration, compelling us to cast aside sin and embrace a deeper love for our Heavenly Father.

With your unparalleled strength and profound humility, we earnestly beseech you to conquer any darkness of evil and pride that may dwell within the depths of our hearts, allowing us to draw nearer to the loving presence of God.

St. Michael the Archangel, we fervently pray for your intercession, that we may be blessed with a profound desire to humble ourselves before our Heavenly Father and wholeheartedly embrace His divine will.

You, the distinguished prince among angels, exemplify humility through your unwavering acknowledgment of God's supreme authority and your wholehearted acceptance of your role as His devoted servant. Unlike Satan, who succumbed to the treacherous allure of pride, you remained steadfast in your humility. We humbly beseech you to guide us in nurturing and cultivating this same profound humility in our own lives.

With hearts filled with the spirit of humility, we present our petitions before you...

(State your petitions)

"Saint Michael the Archangel, valiantly defend us in the midst of our spiritual battles, be our impenetrable shield against the malevolence and cunning snares of the devil. We humbly implore God to rebuke him; and by the boundless power of God, may you, O Prince of the Heavenly host, cast Satan and all malevolent spirits into the depths of hell, where they relentlessly seek the ruin of souls."

Amen.

In the name of the Father, and of the Son, and the Holy Spirit.

Amen.

Day 6

In the name of the Father, and of the Son, and the Holy Spirit.

Amen.

St. Michael the Archangel, we revere you as a powerful protector of the Church and the vigilant guardian of our souls. May your humility, courage, and strength be a perpetual source of inspiration, urging us to turn away from sin and nurture our love for our Heavenly Father.

In your unwavering strength and profound humility, we beseech you to conquer any evil and pride that may lurk within our hearts, ensuring that nothing stands as an obstacle between us and God's boundless grace.

St. Michael the Archangel, we fervently pray for the grace to place unwavering faith in the loving care of our Heavenly Father.

You, the distinguished prince among angels, epitomize humility through your unwavering acknowledgment of God's supreme authority and your wholehearted acceptance of your role as His devoted servant. Unlike Satan, who fell prey to the treacherous allure of pride, you remained steadfast in your humility. Pray that we may cultivate this same profound humility.

With the spirit of humility enkindled within us, we lay our petitions before you...

(State your petitions)

"Saint Michael the Archangel, be our valiant defender in the midst of spiritual battles, our impenetrable shield against the wickedness and cunning snares of the devil. We humbly implore God to rebuke him; and by the boundless power of God, may you, O Prince of the Heavenly host, cast Satan and all malevolent spirits into the depths of hell, where they relentlessly seek the ruin of souls."

Amen.

In the name of the Father, and of the Son, and the Holy Spirit.

Amen.

Day 7

In the name of the Father, and of the Son, and the Holy Spirit.

Amen.

St. Michael the Archangel, we extend our heartfelt homage to you as a mighty guardian of the Church and the vigilant protector of our souls. May your unwavering humility, dauntless courage, and enduring strength remain an eternal source of inspiration, urging us to turn away from sin and nurture our love for our Heavenly Father.

With your unparalleled strength and profound humility, we fervently implore you to conquer any lingering darkness of evil and pride that may hide within the depths of our hearts, ensuring that nothing obstructs our unbreakable bond with God.

St. Michael the Archangel, we earnestly pray for the grace to joyfully dedicate every facet of our lives for the greater glory of God.

You, the distinguished prince among angels, epitomize humility through your unwavering acknowledgment of God's supreme authority and your wholehearted embrace of your role as His devoted servant. Unlike Satan, who fell victim to the treacherous allure of pride, you remained steadfast in your humility. Pray that we may wholeheartedly embrace this same profound humility.

With the spirit of humility kindled within us, we lay our petitions before you...

(State your petitions)

"Saint Michael the Archangel, stand as our valiant defender amidst our spiritual battles, our impenetrable shield against the malevolence and cunning snares of the devil. We humbly implore God to rebuke him; and by the boundless power of God, may you, O Prince of the Heavenly host, cast Satan and all malevolent spirits into the abyss of hell, where they relentlessly seek the ruin of souls."

Amen.

In the name of the Father, and of the Son, and the Holy Spirit.

Amen.

Day 8

In the name of the Father, and of the Son, and the Holy Spirit.

Amen.

St. Michael the Archangel, we hold you in high esteem as a potent guardian of the Church and the vigilant protector of our souls. May your unwavering humility, dauntless courage, and enduring strength serve as an eternal source of inspiration, compelling us to shun sin and perfect our love for our Heavenly Father.

In your unyielding strength and profound humility, we entreat you to vanquish the shadows of evil and pride that may lurk within our hearts, ensuring that nothing severs our sacred connection with God.

St. Michael the Archangel, we fervently beseech you to grant us the resolve to unwaveringly adhere to all of God's commandments.

You, the distinguished prince among angels, epitomize humility through your steadfast acknowledgment of God's supreme dominion and your wholehearted acceptance of your role as His devoted servant. Unlike Satan, who succumbed to the treacherous siren call of pride, you remained resolute in your humility. Pray that we may embrace this same profound humility.

With hearts humbled by the spirit of humility, we present our petitions...

(State your petitions)

"Saint Michael the Archangel, stand as our stalwart defender in the midst of spiritual warfare, our impenetrable shield against the malevolence and crafty snares of the devil. We humbly implore God to rebuke him; and through your formidable power, O Prince of the Heavenly host, cast Satan and all malevolent spirits into the abyss of hell, where they relentlessly seek the ruin of souls."

Amen.

In the name of the Father, and of the Son, and the Holy Spirit.

Amen.

Day 9

In the name of the Father, and of the Son, and the Holy Spirit.

Amen.

St. Michael the Archangel, we humbly offer our deepest homage to you as a mighty guardian of the Church and the unwavering protector of our souls. May your humility, bravery, and strength serve as an everlasting source of inspiration, urging us to turn away from sin and nurture our love for our Heavenly Father.

With your unwavering strength and profound humility, we fervently implore you to conquer any lingering darkness of evil and pride that may hide within the depths of our hearts, ensuring that nothing severs our sacred connection with God.

St. Michael the Archangel, we fervently pray for the grace to share in the eternal glory of our Heavenly Father.

You, the distinguished prince among angels, epitomize humility through your unwavering acknowledgment of God's supreme authority and your wholehearted embrace of your role as His devoted servant. Unlike Satan, who fell victim to the treacherous allure of pride, you remained steadfast in your humility. Pray that we may wholeheartedly embrace this same profound humility.

With humility kindled within our hearts, we lay our petitions before you...

(State your petitions)

"Saint Michael the Archangel, be our unwavering defender amidst the spiritual battles we face, our unbreakable shield against the malevolence and cunning snares of the devil. We humbly implore God to rebuke him; and through your indomitable power, O Prince of the Heavenly host, cast Satan and all malevolent spirits into the abyss of hell, where they relentlessly seek the ruin of souls."

Amen.

In the name of the Father, and of the Son, and the Holy Spirit.

Amen.

Chapter 8: A Litany of St. Michael

Lord, extend your mercy to us. Lord, extend your mercy to us.

Christ, shower your mercy upon us. Christ, shower your mercy upon us.

Lord, shower your mercy upon us. Lord, shower your mercy upon us.

Christ, hear our cries. Christ, hear our cries.

Christ, kindly listen to us. Christ, kindly listen to us.

Heavenly Father, God above, grant us your mercy.

Jesus Christ, the Redeemer of the world, bestow your mercy.

Holy Spirit of God, have mercy on us.

Holy Trinity, one God, pour out your mercy.

[Repeat the following phrases, adding "pray for us" after each one]

Holy Mary, Queen of the Angels,

St. Michael, the Archangel,

Glorious servant of the Triune Divinity,

Standing by the incense-laden altar,

Heavenly Ambassador,

Majestic Leader of the Celestial Armies,

Commander of Angelic Hosts,

Bearer of God's Standard,

Shielder of Divine Majesty,

First Guardian of Christ's Kingship,

Divine Strength,

Unconquerable Prince and Champion,

Bringer of Peace,

Guide of Christ,

Defender of the Catholic Faith,

Advocate of God's People,

Guardian of the Eucharist,

Protector of the Church,

Safeguard of the Supreme Pontiff,

Angel of Catholic Action,

Mighty Intercessor for Christians,

Courageous Protector of those who trust in God,

Guardian of our souls and bodies,

Healer of the infirm,

Comforter of those in their last moments,

Consoler of Souls in Purgatory,

Messenger of God's justice for the just,

Dread of evil spirits,

Triumphant warrior against wickedness,

Guardian and Patron of the entire Church,

Lamb of God, who takes away the sins of the world,

spare us, O Lord.

Lamb of God, who takes away the sins of the world,

graciously hear us, O Lord.

Lamb of God, who takes away the sins of the world,

have mercy on us.

V. Pray for us, O glorious St. Michael,

R. That we may be found worthy of Christ's

promises.

A Solemn Act of Dedication to St. Michael the

Archangel

O illustrious Prince of the Angelic Hierarchies,

courageous warrior of Almighty God,

ardent champion of His glory,

terror to the rebellious angels,

and delight and love of all the righteous,

beloved Archangel Saint Michael,

with a deep desire to be counted among your

devoted followers,

I today consecrate and devote myself to you,

and entrust to your powerful protection myself, my

family,

and all that I possess.

I humbly ask you not to consider my unworthiness

as your servant,

for I am but a miserable sinner,

but let the affection with which I make this offering

persuade you to accept it.

During my entire life and at the hour of my death,

please assist me.

Defend me against the assaults of the infernal

adversary,

especially in the last moments of my life.

Come and rescue me in my final struggle,

and with your mighty sword,

cast into the depths of hell that accuser and proud

angel

whom you overcame in the heavenly battle.

Saint Michael, defend us in our daily combat

so that we may not be lost at the hour of final

judgment.

Chapter 9: The Chaplet of St. Michael

The Chaplet of St. Michael stands as a cherished tribute to honor this Archangel alongside the other nine Celestial Choirs, with the Seraphim as the highest and the Angelic Choir as the lowest.

This devotion, crafted by Antónia de Astónaco, a devout Carmelite nun from Portugal, unfolded through a divine revelation from Archangel Michael himself. In this revelation, she was called to pay homage to the Archangel by offering nine salutations to the nine Choirs of Angels.

Understanding the St. Michael Chaplet

A chaplet, a form of personal devotion, is often recited with the aid of prayer beads, although it can be practiced without them. An example of this is the Rosary. Archangel Michael, renowned as a spiritual warrior and a chief angel of the Church, takes center stage in this devotion.

Unveiling its Historical Roots

The origins of this chaplet trace back to the 18th century and a Servant of God named Antonia d'Astonac. It was during this time that she experienced a divine vision of St. Michael the Archangel. In this vision, St. Michael instructed her to offer nine salutations to the nine Choirs of Angels, promising his protective care along with an angel from each Choir to those who faithfully recite the chaplet. For those who embrace daily prayer of the chaplet, St. Michael and the angels pledge their guidance and safeguarding throughout life and beyond.

The Papal Approval

Pope Pius gave his papal approval to Antonia's vision and the Chaplet of St. Michael in 1851, solidifying its place as a revered form of devotion.

Distinguishing it from the St. Michael Prayer

While the Chaplet enjoys popularity, the shorter St. Michael Prayer stands as one of the most renowned intercessory prayers in the Christian world. It was penned by Pope Leo XIII after a vision he experienced during Mass. This prayer, included below, seeks St. Michael's intercession and protection:

"Saint Michael the Archangel, defend us in battle.

Be our protection against the wickedness and snares

of the devil;

May God rebuke him, we humbly pray;

And do thou, O Prince of the Heavenly Host, by the

power of God, thrust into hell Satan and all evil

spirits who wander through the world for the ruin of

souls. Amen."

Both the prayer and the Chaplet guide us in seeking

the intercession of St. Michael the Archangel in the

spiritual battles we encounter as individuals,

communities, and the Church.

The Significance of Praying the St. Michael Chaplet

The Book of Revelation reveals St. Michael the Archangel as a spiritual warrior, defending us against the forces of evil, particularly Satan. The St. Michael Chaplet serves as a conduit to acknowledge St. Michael's willingness and ability to protect us. It implores his intercession in times of spiritual strife.

Ultimately, we engage in the St. Michael Chaplet to invoke the Archangel's protective presence during our personal battles, to fortify our bodies and souls against the forces of darkness, and to nurture humility by placing our trust in God rather than relying solely on ourselves.

When to Invoke the St. Michael Chaplet?

The St. Michael Chaplet becomes a beacon of solace during moments of distress, fear, or temptation, when words elude us in our plea for divine assistance.

Turn to St. Michael whenever you find yourself embroiled in your personal "battles," and beseech his intercession and protection.

Additionally, mark September 29th, the Feast Day of St. Michael the Archangel, on your calendar as an auspicious occasion to recite this Chaplet.

The Divine Promises of St. Michael the Archangel for Chaplet Devotees

St. Michael the Archangel extends these divine promises to those who faithfully recite the Chaplet of St. Michael:

- Nine angels, each representing the nine Choirs, will accompany the faithful when they approach to receive Holy Communion.
- Consistent daily recitation of the Chaplet of St. Michael ensures ongoing assistance from the Archangel throughout one's lifetime, extending to deliverance from purgatory for both the devotee and their faithful relatives.

Praying the St. Michael Chaplet

Estimated time: 5 minutes

The Procedure for Praying the St. Michael Chaplet

1. Begin by invoking the presence of God.

   O God, come to my assistance. O Lord, make

haste to help me.

   Glory be to the Father, and to the Son, and to the

Holy Spirit. As it was in the beginning, is now, and

ever shall be, world without end.

2. Offer Nine Salutations in reverence to the nine

Choirs of Angels. These Choirs include:

   - Seraphim

   - Cherubim

   - Thrones

- Dominations

- Powers

- Virtues

- Principalities

- Archangels

- Angels

Following each salutation, recite one Our Father and three Hail Marys.

For instance, after the first salutation to the Seraphim, say:

"By the intercession of St. Michael and the celestial Choir of Seraphim, may the Lord make us worthy to burn with the fire of perfect charity. Amen."

3. Offer one Our Father in honor of St. Michael the Archangel.

4. Offer one Our Father in honor of St. Gabriel the Archangel.

5. Offer one Our Father in honor of St. Raphael the Archangel.

6. Offer one Our Father in honor of your Guardian Angel.

7. Conclude your devotional time with God and St. Michael the Archangel by reciting these closing prayers:

"O glorious prince St. Michael, chief and commander of the heavenly hosts, guardian of souls, conqueror of rebel spirits, servant in the house of the Divine King, and our admirable guide, you who shine with excellence and superhuman virtue, deliver us from all evil. We turn to you with confidence, beseeching your gracious protection, that you may enable us to serve God more faithfully with each passing day. Pray for us, O glorious St. Michael, Prince of the Church of Jesus Christ, that we may be found worthy of His promises.

Almighty and Everlasting God, by Your profound goodness and merciful desire for the salvation of all, You have appointed the most glorious Archangel St. Michael as the Prince of Your Church. We implore You to make us worthy, delivering us from all adversaries who would seek

to harass us in the hour of death, and guide us by his

hand into Your Presence. We ask this through the

merits of Jesus Christ, Our Lord. Amen."

Chapter 10: Prayers to St. Michael the Archangel

Prayer for Protection Against Evil

St. Michael the Archangel, we beseech your vigilant guardianship in times of spiritual conflict. Be our impenetrable shield against the malevolent forces and cunning snares of the devil. May we, with humility, entreat the Lord's rebuke upon him. O Prince of the heavenly host, through the might of God, cast into the abyss Satan and all the evil spirits who roam the world, seeking the destruction of souls. Amen.

A Personal Appeal to Saint Michael the Archangel

Dear Saint Michael the Archangel, we earnestly call upon your protective presence during our spiritual battles. May the Lord's rebuke fall upon the malevolent forces, and may you, O Prince of the heavenly host, by God's omnipotent power, bind these malevolent entities and consign them to the sacred fire for their ultimate judgment. Mighty Archangel, disperse darkness, sin, and negativity, ensuring that all that opposes God's radiant light is vanquished. In the name of the Father, the Son, and the Holy Spirit. Amen.

Invocation of Archangel Michael for Guidance

Mighty Archangel Michael, we invoke your guidance and safeguarding throughout our day. Abide by our side, directing our actions and words with love. Cleanse us from pessimism and erroneous beliefs, enabling us to radiate positivity. We offer this prayer in your name. Amen.

Prayer to Archangel Michael for Healing

Healing Angels sent by God through Archangel Michael, we humbly seek your divine presence upon us and our cherished ones. Infuse us with your healing radiance and divine grace, bestowing solace and renewal upon our bodies, minds, and spirits.

Amen.

Prayer to Archangel Michael for Love and Security

Loving God and Archangel Michael, we express gratitude for your watchful care over us and those we cherish. Grant us assurance, serenity, and unwavering faith as we focus on our priorities and strive for a joyful and wholesome existence. In your name, we pray. Amen.

Invocation of Archangel Michael for Courage

Mighty St. Michael, the Archangel, we extol your glorious role as protector and champion of the celestial realms. We implore your special shelter and valor. Empower us with the fortitude to conquer adversities and remain steadfast in our devotion to our Redeemer. Stand with us in moments of peril and temptation, ensuring our triumph over the adversary. In your name, we pray. Amen.

Catholic Prayer for Angelic Guidance

Holy Father, we offer gratitude for the gift of Archangels, entrusted to guide and safeguard us. St. Michael, our guardian, we invoke your vigilance over us and our loved ones, shielding us from harm. St. Gabriel, bearer of glad tidings, assist us in discerning truth and hearing God's voice. St. Raphael, the healing angel, bestow your gifts of restoration upon us and those we cherish. We welcome the presence and intercession of these celestial beings. Holy Angels, pray for us. Amen.

Chapter 11: St. Gabriel the Archangel Novena

Day 1

In the presence of the Father, the Son, and the Holy Spirit, I begin this novena. Amen.

Opening Prayer

St. Gabriel the Archangel, I hold you in profound reverence as the Messenger of the Incarnation. You were chosen by God to deliver divine messages to Daniel, Zechariah, and the Blessed Virgin Mary. Instill within me a deep and fervent love for the Incarnate Word and His Blessed Mother, mirroring your own devotion.

I also honor you as the Giver of God's Strength, bestowing divine fortitude and comfort upon the faithful. Strengthen my resolve, renew my courage, and be my solace and support in the trials of daily life, just as you consoled our Savior in His agony, Mary in her sorrows, and Joseph in his trials. I place my unwavering trust in you.

St. Gabriel, I present this special petition before you: (mention your request here). Through your unwavering devotion to the Son of God and His Blessed Mother, I implore your intercession in alignment with God's holy Will.

Pray for us, St. Gabriel the Archangel, that we may be found deserving of Christ's promises.

Closing Prayer

Almighty and eternal God, in choosing Archangel Gabriel above all others to proclaim the mystery of Your Son's Incarnation, grant that we who honor him on Earth may partake in the rewards of his heavenly patronage. We make this request through Christ our Lord.

Amen.

Day 2

In the presence of the Father, the Son, and the Holy Spirit, I commence this novena. Amen.

Opening Prayer

St. Gabriel the Archangel, I deeply revere you as the Angel of the Incarnation. God entrusted you with the sacred task of delivering messages about the God-Man to Daniel, Zechariah, and the Blessed Virgin Mary. Implant within me a profound and dedicated love for the Incarnate Word and His Blessed Mother, akin to your own devotion.

I also recognize your role as the Source of God's Strength, bestowing divine strength, comfort, and consolation upon God's faithful. I seek the grace of

unyielding determination to lead a life of holiness.

Strengthen my resolutions, rekindle my courage,

and be my solace and support in the trials and

tribulations of everyday life, as you comforted our

Savior in His agony, Mary in her sorrows, and

Joseph in his trials. My trust is firmly placed in you.

St. Gabriel, I present this special request before you:

(mention your request here). Through your

unwavering devotion to the Son of God and His

Blessed Mother, I humbly implore your intercession

in accordance with God's divine Will.

Pray for us, St. Gabriel the Archangel, that we may

be found worthy of Christ's promises.

Closing Prayer

Almighty and eternal God, who chose Archangel
Gabriel above all others to announce the mystery of
Your Son's Incarnation, graciously grant that we,
who honor him on Earth, may share in the blessings
of his heavenly patronage. We beseech this through
Christ our Lord.

Amen.

Day 3

In the presence of the Holy Trinity, I begin this
novena. Amen.

Opening Prayer

St. Gabriel the Archangel, I hold you in profound
reverence as the Angel of the Incarnation. God has
uniquely chosen you to deliver messages about the
God-Man to Daniel, Zechariah, and the Blessed
Virgin Mary. Instill within me a deep and
unwavering love for the Incarnate Word and His
Blessed Mother, a love that mirrors your own.

I also honor you as the Bestower of God's Strength,
the channel of divine fortitude and comfort chosen

to strengthen the faithful and convey essential truths.

I implore the grace of unwavering determination to pursue holiness in my life. Steady my resolve, renew my courage, and offer solace and support in the challenges, trials, and tribulations of daily existence, just as you consoled our Savior in His agony, Mary in her sorrows, and Joseph in his trials. My trust is firmly placed in you.

St. Gabriel, I present this specific request before you: (mention your request here). Through your profound love for the Son of God and His Blessed Mother, I earnestly beseech you to intercede on my behalf, in accordance with God's holy Will.

Pray for us, St. Gabriel the Archangel, that we may be deemed worthy of Christ's promises.

Closing Prayer

Almighty and eternal God, who chose the Archangel Gabriel from among all the angels to proclaim the mystery of Your Son's Incarnation, kindly grant that we, who honor him on Earth, may experience the benefits of his heavenly patronage. We make this request through Christ our Lord.

Amen.

Day 4

In the presence of the Holy Trinity, I embark on this
novena. Amen.

Opening Prayer

St. Gabriel the Archangel, I hold you in profound
reverence as the Angel of the Incarnation. God has
uniquely chosen you to deliver messages about the
God-Man to Daniel, Zechariah, and the Blessed
Virgin Mary. Instill within me a deep and
unwavering love for the Incarnate Word and His
Blessed Mother, a love that mirrors your own.

I also honor you as the Bestower of God's Strength,
the channel of divine fortitude and comfort chosen

to strengthen the faithful and convey essential truths.

I implore the grace of unwavering determination to pursue holiness in my life. Steady my resolve, renew my courage, and offer solace and support in the challenges, trials, and tribulations of daily existence, just as you consoled our Savior in His agony, Mary in her sorrows, and Joseph in his trials. My trust is firmly placed in you.

St. Gabriel, I present this specific request before you: (mention your request here). Through your profound love for the Son of God and His Blessed Mother, I earnestly beseech you to intercede on my behalf, in accordance with God's holy Will.

Pray for us, St. Gabriel the Archangel, that we may be deemed worthy of Christ's promises.

Closing Prayer

Almighty and eternal God, who chose the Archangel Gabriel from among all the angels to proclaim the mystery of Your Son's Incarnation, kindly grant that we, who honor him on Earth, may experience the benefits of his heavenly patronage. We make this request through Christ our Lord.

Amen.

Day 5

In the presence of the Holy Trinity, I commence this day's novena. Amen.

Opening Prayer

St. Gabriel the Archangel, I deeply honor you as the Angel of the Incarnation. God has chosen you uniquely to convey messages about the God-Man to Daniel, Zechariah, and the Blessed Virgin Mary. Infuse within me an abiding and devoted love for the Incarnate Word and His Blessed Mother, a love that mirrors your own.

I also hold you in high regard as the Bestower of God's Strength, the channel of divine fortitude, the consoler, and the comforter chosen to strengthen the faithful and impart vital truths.

I humbly implore the grace of an unwavering will, empowering me to pursue holiness in my life. Steady my resolutions, renew my courage, and provide solace and support in the challenges, trials, and tribulations of daily existence, just as you consoled our Savior in His agony, Mary in her sorrows, and Joseph in his trials. My trust is steadfastly placed in you.

St. Gabriel, I present this particular request before you: (mention your request here). Through your profound love for the Son of God and His Blessed Mother, I earnestly beseech you to intercede on my behalf, in accordance with God's holy Will.

Pray for us, St. Gabriel the Archangel, that we may be found worthy of the promises of Christ.

Closing Prayer

Almighty and eternal God, who chose the Archangel Gabriel from among all the Angels to proclaim the mystery of Your Son's Incarnation, kindly grant that we, who honor him on Earth, may experience the benefits of his heavenly patronage. We make this request through Christ our Lord.

Amen.

Day 6

In the presence of the Holy Trinity, I embark on this day's novena. Amen.

Opening Prayer

St. Gabriel the Archangel, I deeply honor you as the Angel of the Incarnation. God has chosen you uniquely to convey messages about the God-Man to Daniel, Zechariah, and the Blessed Virgin Mary. Infuse within me an abiding and devoted love for the Incarnate Word and His Blessed Mother, a love that mirrors your own.

I also hold you in high regard as the Bestower of God's Strength, the channel of divine fortitude, the consoler, and the comforter chosen to strengthen the faithful and impart vital truths.

I humbly implore the grace of an unwavering will, empowering me to pursue holiness in my life. Steady my resolutions, renew my courage, and provide solace and support in the challenges, trials, and tribulations of daily existence, just as you consoled our Savior in His agony, Mary in her sorrows, and Joseph in his trials. My trust is steadfastly placed in you.

St. Gabriel, I present this particular request before you: (mention your request here). Through your profound love for the Son of God and His Blessed Mother, I earnestly beseech you to intercede on my behalf, in accordance with God's holy Will.

Pray for us, St. Gabriel the Archangel, that we may be found worthy of the promises of Christ.

Closing Prayer

Almighty and eternal God, who chose the Archangel Gabriel from among all the Angels to proclaim the mystery of Your Son's Incarnation, kindly grant that we, who honor him on Earth, may experience the benefits of his heavenly patronage. We make this request through Christ our Lord.

Amen.

Day 7

In the name of the Holy Trinity, I begin this seventh day of our novena. Amen.

Opening Prayer

St. Gabriel the Archangel, I hold you in profound reverence as the Angel of the Incarnation. God has uniquely chosen you to convey messages about the God-Man to Daniel, Zechariah, and the Blessed Virgin Mary. Instill within me a profound and unwavering love for the Incarnate Word and His Blessed Mother, a love that mirrors your own.

I also honor you as the Bestower of God's Strength, the bearer of divine fortitude, the consoler, and the comforter chosen to strengthen the faithful and impart essential truths.

I beseech you for the grace of an unshakable will, empowering me to pursue holiness in my life. Steady my resolutions, renew my courage, and provide comfort and solace in the face of challenges, trials, and tribulations, just as you consoled our Savior in His agony, Mary in her sorrows, and Joseph in his trials. I place my trust entirely in you.

St. Gabriel, I now present this specific request before you: (mention your request here). Through your profound love for the Son of God and His Blessed Mother, I earnestly implore you to intercede on my behalf, in accordance with God's holy Will.

Pray for us, St. Gabriel the Archangel, that we may be deemed worthy of Christ's promises.

Closing Prayer

Almighty and eternal God, who chose the Archangel Gabriel from among all the Angels to proclaim the mystery of Your Son's Incarnation, we beseech You to graciously grant that we, who honor Him on Earth, may experience the benefits of His heavenly patronage. We make this request through Christ our Lord.

Amen.

Day 8

In the name of the Holy Trinity, I commence this eighth day of our novena. Amen.

Opening Prayer

St. Gabriel the Archangel, I hold you in veneration as the Angel of the Incarnation, for God has specially chosen you to convey messages about the God-Man to Daniel, Zechariah, and the Blessed Virgin Mary. Grant me a deep and devoted love for the Incarnate Word and His Blessed Mother, resembling your own.

I also honor you as the Source of God's Strength, as you bestow divine strength, console, and comfort upon God's faithful, and impart essential truths to them.

I humbly request the grace of a special strength of will to pursue holiness in life. Steady my resolutions, renew my courage, and provide comfort and solace during the challenges, trials, and tribulations of daily living, as you consoled our Savior in His agony, Mary in her sorrows, and Joseph in his trials. I place my trust in you.

St. Gabriel, I now present this specific request before you: (mention your request here). Through your fervent love for the Son of God and His Blessed Mother, I implore you to intercede on my behalf, in accordance with God's holy Will.

Pray for us, St. Gabriel the Archangel, that we may be considered worthy of the promises of Christ.

Closing Prayer

Almighty and everlasting God, as You chose the Archangel Gabriel from among all the Angels to announce the mystery of Your Son's Incarnation, we beseech You to graciously allow us, who honor Him on Earth, to experience the benefits of His patronage in Heaven. We make this request through Christ our Lord.

Amen.

Day 9

In the presence of the Holy Trinity, I commence this ninth day of our novena. Amen.

Opening Prayer

St. Gabriel the Archangel, I hold you in profound reverence as the Angel of the Incarnation. God has uniquely chosen you to deliver messages about the God-Man to Daniel, Zechariah, and the Blessed Virgin Mary. Infuse within me a profound and unwavering love for the Incarnate Word and His Blessed Mother, a love that reflects your own.

I also honor you as the Bestower of God's Strength, the channel of divine strength, the consoler, and comforter chosen to strengthen the faithful and convey vital truths.

I earnestly implore the grace of unwavering willpower to pursue holiness in my life. Steady my resolutions, renew my courage, and provide comfort and solace amid the challenges, trials, and tribulations of daily existence, just as you consoled our Savior in His agony, Mary in her sorrows, and Joseph in his trials. My trust remains steadfast in you.

St. Gabriel, I now present this specific request before you: (mention your request here). Through your profound love for the Son of God and His Blessed Mother, I implore you to intercede on my behalf, in accordance with God's holy Will.

Pray for us, St. Gabriel the Archangel, that we may be deemed worthy of Christ's promises.

Closing Prayer

Almighty and eternal God, having chosen the Archangel Gabriel from among all the Angels to proclaim the mystery of Your Son's Incarnation, we beseech You to kindly allow us, who honor Him on Earth, to partake in the benefits of His heavenly patronage. We make this request through Christ our Lord.

Amen.

Chapter 12: Litany to St. Gabriel

Lord, in Your mercy, we implore,

Christ, graciously hear us once more.

Divine Father in Heaven's abode,

Have mercy on us, the path You've showed.

God the Son, world's Redeemer and Light,

Have mercy, guide us through day and night.

God the Holy Spirit's sanctifying grace,

Have mercy, lead us in Your embrace.

Holy Trinity, One God of might,

Have mercy, guide us toward the light.

Holy Mary, Queen among the Angelic host,

Pray for us, be with us the most.

Saint Gabriel, Archangel so bright,

Intercede for us with your holy might.

Strength of God, we humbly implore,

Stand by our side forevermore.

Gabriel, before God's throne, you stand,

A model of prayer, at His command.

Herald of the wondrous Incarnation story,

Revealing God's glory and heavenly glory.

Prince of Heaven, you hold a place,

Ambassador of the Almighty's grace.

Guardian of the Immaculate's pure soul,

In your care, she reached her heavenly goal.

Foreteller of Jesus' greatness and love,

You descended from Heaven above.

Light of souls and peace's envoy,

Scourge of unbelief, proclaiming joy.

Teacher, you inspire, you instruct,

With wisdom, faith, and truth you conduct.

Protector of the righteous and the meek,

Faithful guardian of those who seek.

First adorer of the Divine Word's birth,

Defender of the Faith on Earth.

Zealous for Jesus' honor so true,

We pray, dear Gabriel, to you we accrue.

Scriptures praise you, God's messenger so bright,

To Mary, the Virgin, you brought Heaven's light.

Lamb of God, who takes sin's weight away,

Grant us mercy, we earnestly pray.

Christ, hear us now, our humble call,

With grace, be near us, guard over all.

Pray for us, blessed Archangel, we beseech,

That Christ's promises, through you, we may reach.

Let us now pray, in this sacred space,

To Archangel Gabriel, seek His grace:

O blessed Archangel Gabriel, dear,

Intercede for us, let us draw near.

At the throne of Divine Mercy's place,

Guide us through life's challenging race.

As you revealed to Mary, the holy decree,

Of the Incarnation, grace so free.

Through your prayers, help us find our way,

And in God's presence forever we'll stay.

Amen.

Chapter 13: Novena

Prayers to St. Raphael

Day 1

In the sacred names of the Father, the Son, and the Holy Spirit, we begin.

Opening Prayer

Majestic Archangel Saint Raphael, distinguished prince of the celestial realm, your wisdom and grace are legendary. You light the path for those who voyage on land, sea, or in the sky, offering solace to the distressed and sanctuary to sinners. I implore your aid in all my trials and tribulations, just as you once aided the young Tobias on his odyssey.

As God's divine remedy, I humbly beseech you to mend the numerous ailments afflicting my soul and body. I particularly request the favor (insert your plea here) and the profound purity necessary to become the dwelling of the Holy Spirit.

Amen.

Closing Prayer

St. Raphael, one of the magnificent seven who stand before the throne of the Living One, Angel of healing, you hold heavenly balm in your hand to soothe and cure our afflictions. Mend the suffering souls and illuminate our way when we tread

uncertain paths.

Day 2

In the name of the Father, the Son, and the Holy Spirit, we invoke divine presence.

Opening Prayer

Glorious Archangel Saint Raphael, eminent prince of the celestial court, renowned for your wisdom and grace, you guide travelers on land, sea, and through the skies, offering solace to the distressed and sanctuary to sinners. Assist me in my needs and tribulations, as you did for the young Tobias on his journey.

As the divine medicine of God, I earnestly beseech you to heal the afflictions of my soul and body. I specially request the favor (state your request here) and the profound purity essential to make me a dwelling for the Holy Spirit.

Amen.

Closing Prayer

St. Raphael, among the resplendent seven who stand in the presence of the One who lives and reigns, Angel of health, your hand overflows with heavenly ointment to alleviate our suffering. Bring healing to the afflicted and steer us when we are uncertain of our path.

Day 3

In the name of the Father, the Son, and the Holy Spirit, we begin our prayers.

Opening Prayer

Glorious Archangel Saint Raphael, illustrious prince of the heavenly realm, celebrated for your wisdom and grace, you guide those on journeys by land, sea, or air, providing solace to the afflicted and refuge to sinners. Aid me in my needs and tribulations, just as you did for the young Tobias during his travels.

As God's divine remedy, I humbly implore you to heal the afflictions of my soul and body. I specifically seek the favor (mention your request here) and the profound purity required to prepare me as a sanctuary for the Holy Spirit.

Amen.

Closing Prayer

St. Raphael, one of the illustrious seven who stand before the throne of the Living One, Angel of health, the Lord has entrusted you with heavenly balm to alleviate or cure our suffering. Bring healing to the afflicted and illuminate our way when doubts cloud our path.

Day 4

In the name of the Father, the Son, and the Holy Spirit, we invoke divine blessings.

Opening Prayer

Glorious Archangel Saint Raphael, distinguished prince of the heavenly court, renowned for your wisdom and grace, you guide those on journeys by land, sea, or air, offering solace to the afflicted and sanctuary to sinners. Assist me in all my needs and tribulations, as you once aided the young Tobias during his travels.

As the divine medicine of God, I humbly implore you to heal the afflictions of my soul and body. I especially request the favor (mention your request here) and the profound grace of purity needed to prepare me as a temple for the Holy Spirit.

Amen.

Closing Prayer

St. Raphael, among the glorious seven who stand in the presence of the One who lives and reigns, Angel of health, the Lord has entrusted you with heavenly balm to soothe or cure our suffering. Bring healing to the afflicted and guide our steps when uncertainty clouds our way.

Day 5

In the sacred names of the Father, the Son, and the
Holy Spirit, we gather in prayer.

Opening Invocation

Majestic Archangel Saint Raphael, distinguished
prince of the celestial court, renowned for your
wisdom and grace, you illuminate the path for
travelers by land, sea, and air. You console the
afflicted and provide refuge for sinners. I implore
your guidance in all my needs and the trials of this
life, just as you once aided young Tobias on his
journey.

As God's divine remedy, I humbly beseech you to mend the numerous infirmities that afflict my soul and body. I especially request the favor (insert your plea here) and the profound grace of purity to sanctify me as a dwelling for the Holy Spirit.

Amen.

Concluding Benediction

St. Raphael, among the resplendent seven who stand before the throne of the Living One, Angel of healing, your hand holds celestial balm to soothe our suffering. Bring healing to those afflicted and light the way for us when doubt shrouds our path.

Day 6

In the name of the Father, the Son, and the Holy Spirit, we come together in prayer.

Opening Invocation

Glorious Archangel Saint Raphael, eminent prince of the heavenly court, renowned for your wisdom and grace, you guide those who journey by land, sea, or air. You offer solace to the afflicted and refuge to sinners. I implore your assistance in all my needs and the tribulations of this life, just as you once aided young Tobias on his travels.

As the divine medicine of God, I earnestly seek your healing touch for the afflictions of my soul and body. I specially request the favor (state your request here) and the profound purity required to make me a temple for the Holy Spirit.

Amen.

Concluding Benediction

St. Raphael, among the illustrious seven who stand in the presence of the One who lives and reigns, Angel of health, your hand overflows with heavenly ointment to alleviate our suffering. Bring healing to those in need and guide our steps when uncertainty clouds our way.

Day 7

In the name of the Father, the Son, and the Holy
Spirit, we join in prayer.

Opening Invocation

Glorious Archangel Saint Raphael, illustrious prince
of the heavenly realm, celebrated for your wisdom
and grace, you guide travelers on land, sea, and
through the skies, offering solace to the afflicted
and sanctuary to sinners. Assist me in my needs and
tribulations, as you did for young Tobias during his
travels.

As God's divine remedy, I humbly implore you to
heal the afflictions of my soul and body. I

specifically seek the favor (mention your request here) and the profound purity essential to prepare me as a sanctuary for the Holy Spirit.

Amen.

Concluding Benediction

St. Raphael, one of the illustrious seven who stand before the throne of the Living One, Angel of health, the Lord has entrusted you with heavenly balm to alleviate or cure our suffering. Bring healing to those in distress and illuminate our way when doubts cloud our path.

Day 8

In the name of the Father, the Son, and the Holy Spirit, we gather in prayer.

Opening Invocation

Glorious Archangel Saint Raphael, distinguished prince of the heavenly court, renowned for your wisdom and grace, you guide those who journey by land, sea, or air. You offer consolation to the afflicted and refuge to sinners. I beg your assistance in all my needs and the tribulations of this life, just as you once helped young Tobias on his travels.

As the divine medicine of God, I humbly implore you to heal the afflictions of my soul and body. I especially request the favor (mention your request here) and the great grace of purity to prepare me as a temple for the Holy Spirit.

Amen.

Concluding Benediction

St. Raphael, among the glorious seven who stand in the presence of the One who lives and reigns, Angel of health, the Lord has filled your hand with balm from heaven to soothe or cure our pains. Heal those suffering and guide our steps when doubt shadows our way.

Day 9

In the sacred names of the Father, the Son, and the Holy Spirit, we unite in prayer.

Opening Invocation

Majestic Archangel Saint Raphael, eminent prince of the heavenly realm, renowned for your wisdom and grace, you illuminate the path for travelers on land, sea, or in the skies. You console the afflicted and offer refuge to sinners. I implore your guidance in all my needs and the trials of this life, just as you once aided young Tobias on his journey.

As God's divine remedy, I humbly entreat you to heal the numerous afflictions that beset my soul and body. I specially seek the favor (insert your plea here) and the profound grace of purity to sanctify me as a dwelling for the Holy Spirit.

Amen.

Concluding Benediction

St. Raphael, among the resplendent seven who stand before the throne of the Living One, Angel of healing, your hand holds celestial balm to soothe our suffering. Bring healing to those in need and light the way for us when doubt obscures our path.

Chapter 14: Litany of St. Raphael

Lord, have mercy on us.

 Christ, have mercy on us.

Lord, have mercy on us. Christ, hear our prayer.

Christ, graciously hear us.

God the Father of Heaven,

Have mercy on us.

God the Son, Redeemer of the world,

Have mercy on us.

God the Holy Spirit,

Have mercy on us.

Holy Trinity, One God,

Have mercy on us.

Holy Mary, Queen of Angels,

pray for us.

St. Raphael,

pray for us.

St. Raphael, vessel of God's mercy,

pray for us.

St. Raphael, devoted adorer of the Divine Word,

pray for us.

St. Raphael, vanquisher of evil forces,

pray for us.

St. Raphael, guardian against vice,

pray for us.

St. Raphael, source of healing for the infirm,

pray for us.

St. Raphael, our refuge in trials,

pray for us.

St. Raphael, guiding light for travelers,

pray for us.

St. Raphael, solace for those in captivity,

pray for us.

St. Raphael, bringer of joy to the sorrowful,

pray for us.

St. Raphael, zealous for souls' salvation,

pray for us.

St. Raphael, bearer of the name "God heals,"

pray for us.

St. Raphael, champion of purity,

pray for us.

St. Raphael, banisher of malevolent spirits,

pray for us.

St. Raphael, in times of disease, hunger, and
conflict,

pray for us.

St. Raphael, Angel of peace and prosperity,

pray for us.

St. Raphael, endowed with the gift of healing,

pray for us.

St. Raphael, sure guide on the path to virtue and

holiness,

pray for us.

St. Raphael, aid to all who seek your help,

pray for us.

St. Raphael, who guided and comforted Tobias on

his journey,

pray for us.

St. Raphael, praised in Scripture as "Raphael, the

holy Angel of the Lord, was sent to heal,"

pray for us.

St. Raphael, our intercessor,

pray for us.

Lamb of God, Who takes away the sins of the world,

    Spare us, O Lord.

Lamb of God, Who takes away the sins of the world,

    Graciously hear us, O Lord.

Lamb of God, Who takes away the sins of the world,

    Have mercy on us.

Christ, hear us.

    Christ, graciously hear us.

Pray for us, St. Raphael, before the throne of the Lord Our God,

That we may be deemed worthy of Christ's promises.

Let Us Pray.

Lord Jesus Christ, through the intercession of the Archangel Raphael, grant us the grace to shun sin and persist in every virtuous endeavor until we attain our heavenly destination. You who reign forever and ever. Amen.

Printed in Great Britain
by Amazon

40818887R00106